Sonets from the Chesapeke

Stephen Evans

"What do we know but that we face
One another in this place?"

W. B. Yeats

This is a work of poetic fiction. The names,
characters, places, and incidents are either
the products of the author's imagination or
are used fictitiously, and any resemblance to
actual persons living or dead, business
establishments, events, or locales is entirely
coincidental.

Sonets from the Chesapeke/Stephen Evans—Third Edition

ISBN: 978-1-953725-38-7

Time Being Media LLC.

CONTENTS

PROLOGUE

I found (or maybe invented) this form years ago. It fits me and my short attention span.

I have lived most of my life near the Chesapeake Bay, spent summers growing up on it's waters, lived for a decade in Annapolis, Maryland, where the Severn River flows into the Bay (we always capitalize it, as if it were the only one). I have used the antique form of the name for my title, because so many of these poems are inspired by memories.

I call these American Sonets because they are a reflection of Americans (as I see us). Americans are Odd, so the stanzas have five lines. Impatient, so the form has twelve lines, not fourteen, and one less letter in the name. Driven, so the meter is iambic. Uneven, so sometimes there are three, four, five feet to the line. Diverse, so some rhyme, some don't. Bold, so a couplet completes the thought.

Sometimes I am all of these too. So these sonets are a reflection of me.

STEPHEN EVANS

GÖDEL'S DREAM

Poetry says what can't be said.
Everything else is prose.
Poetry can't be parsed or pricked.
Just smear it over the eyes and skin
and then inhale, but not too deep.

Poetry isn't verse, nor verse,
poetry. Verse is technique.
Poetry is epistemology.
In your heart you know this,
If you know this in your heart.

Nothing on this page is poetry.
All Cretans are lyres.

STEPHEN EVANS

Time/Life

Not a river, not a stream.
Just a bubble, effervescent
surface with a slender sheen,
Interior beyond descent,
Yet bursting at the seam.

Not a journey, not between,
Just a glimmer of content
Tucked into a mirror seen
At an angle oddly bent,
Yet curiously keen.

This time of life unspent,
a dream I wish I'd seen.

STEPHEN EVANS

Now Then

Now then, the thing about Time Is,
That everything that Isn't
Is an equal distance
from everything that Is.
Now then,

A moment or a year, it doesn't matter,
It's just as far from not to where we are.
I have traveled there and back
to near to here, to hear
Now then,

Where we are to not is just a flash
The momentary sigh from ash to ash.

STEPHEN EVANS

ROMA

Suppose someday, some later time, I stand
In the eternal Roma, beneath, you know,
The Parthenon. No. Get it right. No.
The other one. The. Palladium. No. No.
Pantheon. Yes. That's it. Pantheon.

Beneath the Pantheon I shall stand, gazing
At the gods and goddesses. Are they
Still there? I believe they are. And stand
Gazing. How will I feel? In that ancient
Place?Among that Pantheon of old?

Old but not eternal is how. I.
As they return my gaze with stony eye.

STEPHEN EVANS

MAGI

To come so far still searching
Is disconcerting at the least.
We are travelers from the ancient days.
We follow a star we ourselves set ablaze
and lofted in the skies.

Doggedly we follow, till our eyes,
night-blinded from the launching site,
see burning stars in each celestial turn
and reality is retinality.
We urge each other on from lurch to lurch.

Another thought occurs. When vision clears,
kneel to whichever god is near.

STEPHEN EVANS

The Wine Dark Sea

Where should we go? Sail the wine dark sea?
A sea as dark as wine appeals to me.
A sea composed of wine? Where is the swell
That lofts us to a generous farewell?
That is the sea on which I long to dwell.

Wine dark is not a color but a state.
Blind Homer and I surely can relate.
Wine dark is winter bitter, thunder sweet,
labyrinthine damp, and yet arete,
where vinegar and veneration meet.

Drink up, drink down, drink fearlessly
In endless tidal salty memory.

STEPHEN EVANS

MENTALITY

I haven't seen you lately. But I hope
You don't conclude that I have ceased to think
Of you. You're in my mind, just as I am.
You may be sorry that you ended there,
As am I too, but there you see we are.

Thoughts go swooping by us constantly.
I recommend avoidance. I just duck.
Once they strike there's no escaping them
and then I am afraid per se you're stuck.
As I am. But I cannot cure

This mentality. Instead I send
Profound regrets to you, my mindful friend.

STEPHEN EVANS

THE SEA AS GREEN

I am an island on a sea of grief.
Green! I mean Green. Not grief. I don't mean grief.
I mean. How sad. To be. I mean. You know.
To be an island on a sea of grief.
I mean. You know. How would you get off?

Most islands are volcanoes anyway.
Except big ones like Greenland, which are ice
But maybe have volcanoes underneath.
You never know. But still. The grieving sea.
Who could float on that? You'd have to fly.

Somewhere in the sky there is an eye
That sees the sea as green.

STEPHEN EVANS

SUPPOSE

Suppose that someone loved you. Let us say
That someone does. Did. Anyway.
Suppose that in some future he would say,
or mention once, the love that used to be,
How would you feel? Pretend that it was me.

Suppose you were pretending it was me
That mentioned once the love that used to be,
Would it be easier to turn away?
Or harder? Would it matter? Would you say?
I'm curious. Just curious. Today

I thought of somebody I know, you see,
In such a just supposing sort of way.

STEPHEN EVANS

THE BEATING HEART

Somewhere there's a heart that beats for you.
It isn't mine. Oh no. Oh no. Oh no.
It isn't mine. But I can comprehend
Why someone possibly could possibly
love a person like possibly yourself.

Quietly would sound this nameless heart.
Though hearts are mostly nameless aren't they?
I mean you wouldn't name your body parts,
That would be weird. What would you call yours?
Mine? Ha ha. I'm kidding. No I'm kidding.

But I wonder when I am alone
If one can hear a heart that beats for one.

STEPHEN EVANS

O

O I would write a poem that starts with O
Like Will or Walt. Or one of the Brownings.
Elizabeth or the other one. You know.
Wrote of duchesses and such. O

Maybe you would read it and you'd say
"O he is such a man as writes a poem
That starts with O. I must love him. O
I must. Such men are rare these days. Indeed.
Such men are rare." You are my duchess. O

Maybe you wouldn't read it anyway.
Browning married. Whitman didn't. O.

STEPHEN EVANS

A LITTLE GONE

I'm a little gone with you not here.
I still breathe and everything. And
Even when you go I disappear
Only a bit. Only. A bit more
Each time. Slowly. But sure. Sure.

I sound Irish don't I? Sure. Sure.
That is something you would surely say.
Or surely. Don't call me surely. Ha! There
Was a funny movie. Laughed that day.
We laughed and laughed. Surely. Sure. Sure.

With you not here I am sure a little gone.
And what of me is left is surely done.

STEPHEN EVANS

THE CROSSING

What crossed your mind as I declared my love?

When we were talking. Well, I was talking.

You were. What were you? Listening?

Possibly. I'm not sure you were.

Your eyes were—I can never tell

What's going on inside you from your eyes.

Your mouth was, actually, truthfully, I don't
                                 know.

I cannot look at them and try to talk.

I would just stare. The world ends at your lips.

Your posture though was steady. Not as if

You were going to run away. Of that I'm sure.

What crossed your mind? I'd love. To know. I'd
love.

STEPHEN EVANS

TO THE CHILD I NEVER HAD

I don't know what happened. Or what didn't.
I wish I did. I don't. I wish I did.
Of course I know what didn't. In that way.
I hope that you are happy where you are.
I hope you are. Are you? Are you happy?

To tell the truth, myself (there's no one else,
So why not tell), I often dream, not you,
Not only, but the life I might have,
if you had, if only, in that other.
If we. But I can't see. I can't. See you.

To the child I never had. To you. To you.
Do you dream of me? Don't. Be happy.

STEPHEN EVANS

Nocturnal Rendezvous

Do not come too near me yet;
Not while my eye still catches
A glint of sunlight on your hair.
Distance and darkness beautify us all,
While close proximity may cause

The truest love to fail.
Though far away a mountain's
Golden summit we admire,
Up close there's only rock and earth,
Hardly fuel for passion's fire.

I love you for your beauty—
Therefore come to me by night.

STEPHEN EVANS

THE WORLD SAYS

The World says: No one will understand.
No one will ever know what you have done
Or ever read a word that you have written.
When you are gone, your work will be forgotten
And every sign that you have lived will fade.

I say: Hmmm. Let me think. Yep,
That sounds right. I expect nothing
Less than complete oblivion. In fact, I'm
Counting on it. My work is mine, not yours.
Ha ha. So there. The world pauses, thinking.

Then says. Hmmm. Perhaps I was too hasty.
I say: Available through your local bookstore.

STEPHEN EVANS

THE PATH

I walked the path that led me here,
Awhile by choice, a while by chance.
I kept a decent pace for all of that,
On average anyway, especially
For someone who keeps walking looking back.

Some walked with me a little while,
Then turned off, following a different way.
I miss some of them now and then,
And wonder what they saw (in me?)
That sent them spinning off, colliding

Like the moon into the earth, and then away.
I see her still, shining there, until.

S<small>TEPHEN</small> E<small>VANS</small>

Paris

I have not been to Paris, the old man says.
I lived instead inside these little words
That never kept the rain from off my head
Or filtering down the rounded spectacles
That I have always worn, because you must

In a house entirely made of words.
The lenses must be round and thick enough
To speed the water dripping from the rain.
One only hopes refraction won't delay
Gently laying the next rhetorical brick.

A large supply of tissues comes in handy
For drops of rain, or mist, or tears, or brandy.

STEPHEN EVANS

SHALL

Shall I explore the heights of life
Or dive into the depths of me?
That is the question, which remains,
Maybe the only, actually,
And one that causes me some strife.

Somewhere in the strains of death
That beckon toward the dark or light
I hear a different tune that plays
Not yet not never but not yet
And promises a bit more breath.

Shall I play? Without a doubt.
And what remains? Leap and find out.

STEPHEN EVANS

TO A FRIEND WHO
LOST A FRIEND

I see you there. I know that you

Don't want me in that pit with you.

Anyway I'm coming down.

Not to worry. I have a plan.

I'm just going to sit with you

Silent in the healing dark

And watch the languid sun ignore

And the indifferent stars revolve.

I'll be there, as you slowly slip

From stage to stage to stage. And then

When you are ready, I'm your ladder.

Climb, then help me up, my friend.

STEPHEN EVANS

CLIMB

Climb up the steps of love;
Don't vault at once to the roof,
but slowly ascend
in descending slowly
into one another.

Reach (not Paradise)
Each other, and through,
To others you will be,
Greeting each and saying,
"I will love you in your time."

Mark each in memory,
with a certain joy.

STEPHEN EVANS

ZOE'S LAMENT

He wore a crown of crimson imagery
and little else. Why? I never knew.
I chased him 'round that silly tree,
long withered and storm broken, true.
Funny how I grew to love it too.

Once I caught him by the sea
and stripped from him that imagery
and tried to love him, but he lay
pretending to be someday, soon, someday.
I knelt there in the sand. He swam away.

Unmoving, moved, I watched my shadow grow
till somewhere in the sand was strength to go.

STEPHEN EVANS

STARRY SKY

We shall remember you, the world and I,
And write your name across the evening sky.
The world shall write in sunsets, I in stars,
The world shall write you whole, and I in parts,
Because the sky cannot hold all my heart.

The world will then forget you. I will not.
The world forgets what's written. Only what
is loved is remembered. Only what is loved.
The old high way and all, that I strove
Et cetera. Where is the sign? Where is the proof?

The stars behind the sunsets still are there,
Even though you may not be aware.

STEPHEN EVANS

WINTER SKY

To live aboard in winter is not so
Easy. Nothing stems the frigid flow
And cold creeps in from stern to bow
And hail is hell on bright work, as is snow.
Yet here I am, with no place else to go.

Ice has stoned the waves, and I remain
Frozen in this fragile brittle plain,
Afraid to move, or never move again.
The bulkhead groans from the relentless strain
Of closure, of entrapment, in the main.

But still in winter is the yielding sky
That holds more stars than I can wonder why.

STEPHEN EVANS

FREQUENCY

The stars are brighter when the night is cold.
The frigid air is tender to the light,
The dimming shimmer held in check,
Not even gravity disrupts the stream,
Nor truth, aboard the shifting sifting beam,

So ancient, knowing nothing, day or night,
Reaching out, wishing that they could
Finally stop, but finding mostly nothing,
Vast and empty, yet moving fast. Too swift
To understand. That's what happens if

You seek out only with a damaged art,
Where even stars take emptiness to heart.

STEPHEN EVANS

JANUARY

Geese are heading north.
What do they know? What?
Angled wings ignite
The chary sun, fleet
Afire. They know. They know.

Another log on the fire.
That's our wisdom. Burn
until the earth is hot.
Burn until it's not.
Burn. All hope forgot.

What do they know up there
That we do not? Descent.

STEPHEN EVANS

RAIN

Rain only falls in one direction.
You never see it falling up.
Even in the wind, it's going down,
Just taking longer. As if the ground
were happiness, or heaven, or home.

Now wind can blow in any direction.
But wind has neither happiness nor home.
Wind itself is heaven of itself
For motion is a kind of paradise
And heaven never looks behind.

I think I'd rather be the wind than rain;
Heaven without happiness or home.

STEPHEN EVANS

THUNDERSTORMS

Love the luxury of thunderstorms:
Ionic brittle air, refreshing as razors.
Trees that bow as grasses emulate.
Breathe in. Appreciate the thrust
And tumble in the rumblatious air.

That's the point. If there is a point.
But here's a question. Answer if you can.
While we watch and listen and inhale,
Are the many many many drops
That key the many many many leaves,

An algorithm in the code of God,
Each storm a prayer, to Heaven, from this Life?

STEPHEN EVANS

IN WINTER RAIN

In Winter rain, the birds are flying
Branch to branch, tree to naked tree.
I can't help wonder why.
Why this one flies to that?
Why those descend to there?

Are they seeking shelter
In the memory of leaves?
Do they console the trees?
Or do they think
to bring back Spring

By force of will?
Persephone in flight.

STEPHEN EVANS

THE RUSH

There's something in the sound, I guess,
That gushes down the stream,
Feeding the flow that was its genesis,
Or faster maybe, leading, like the beam
From a flashlight in the darkness

To me, as I sit listening, only,
Listening to the waterfall.
Nothing else, just there, just barely there,
Or maybe not at all, and listening,
Hearing, not even that, awash,

Surrounded by the gift
Of softly stumbling air.

STEPHEN EVANS

THE VANISHING STREAM

The thunderstorm donates its wares
On highly indiscriminate grounds
Till finally in the slight depression
Where the reeling hills converge
The rivulet begins

Then quickly vanishes. And yet
If I were thirsty I'd wait there
As whispering clouds discretely gather
Circulate and merge before
Dispensing life.

I'm always thirsty,
Always waiting.

STEPHEN EVANS

THE LITTLE BEACH

The sound returns in half a dream.
The slow sleek prow crunches the shore,
The anchor sinks full fathom deep,
And off I jump to pull her in
And tie her to a tree.

She the captain neatly sets
The tent pegs into easy ground
And with a gesture lifts the shelter
As I roam the sand to gather
Driftwood for a fire.

Returning once again I find
There's nothing there but Summer.

STEPHEN EVANS

WINK WINK

The trees, I thought, were winking
at me early this morning,
tiny bright lights flashing
on and off as if
a child were flipping a switch,

erratic, like a cipher.
I finally figured it out.
The solution was the sunlight
swirling through the dewdrops
as leaves stirred in the breeze.

Nature speaks to us in code.
In time I hope we'll understand.

STEPHEN EVANS

EVENING WALK

The slant of evening light brings clarity.
Emerald silhouetted leaves quake
against the lustered sky while folded
wings congregate in glimmered shelters,
light and shadow tangled in the branches.

The path curves, and we, dimmer now,
and chill, moving closer, hand to hand,
turn knowingly to shelter and repose,
retrace redux the same familiar way
that we have taken every single day,

though somewhere farther on we see
shivered light spill vivid evergreen.

STEPHEN EVANS

NIGHT OF THE HARVEST

Night of the harvest I dive in,
swimming toward the bay.
The moon rented the creek for the night
But didn't mind our play
Or wouldn't say

If it did. The water warm
from the day, still, still
in the calm, stars shuttered
at the moon's will,
and ours, until

you. We float, touch, hold, part,
Within the gravity of absent stars.

STEPHEN EVANS

The Architecture of Trees

How do the branches
know how to grow?
Complexity theory?
Fibonacci Sequences?
Artificial intelligence?

In searching for light,
the branch serves the tree.
What does the branch
know of the tree?
The branch does not look back.

Yet always the same result:
Spare beauty against blue.

STEPHEN EVANS

BLOOM

My azalea is a world unto itself.
But I don't need a telescope to see
The tiny denizens who hide beneath
The tethered cover of the leaves,
Dun-streaked feathered heads declaring
Their domain extends from branch to branch.

I hear that they are mostly colorblind.
I wonder how they see the orange blooms
In that blessed week or two in May
Startling on the verdant branch, where
I am always grateful, and reminded

That all things bloom. They must. Surely they must,
Though we are blind to colors, dust to dust.

STEPHEN EVANS

HIS JOY

Toss a coin into a lake. Go ahead.

Just please be sure to miss the (friendly) fish.

They were there first. If you wish to wait

until the wave is gone, get comfortable.

It's never gone, just beyond your sight.

His joy was like a wave,

Splash like laughter, washing,

Flowing all directions

Was all we saw, all we could see.

But I'll tell you—this I know.

Such joy in life could never dissipate.

Touch the water. Hear it laugh.

STEPHEN EVANS

WHAT IS LEFT

Toss a pebble in a pond.
A ripple swims to shore.
The wave descends. What is left?
The type of influence
And nothing more.

Toss a pond into a pebble
The fluid is a bore.
In the shards, what is left?
The influence of type
And nothing more.

Water and stone, stone and water,
Are what is left to matter.

STEPHEN EVANS

Voice

The voice of the cardinal echoes off the houses.
Every way I turn he's somewhere else,
Red in green, veiled in the host, voice
Sharp as diamonds, silvered pure as stars,
Hosanna fire lost at large. But

Close your eyes. Close them. There. No there
He is, laughing (in a nice way) at the
Dizzy human, with such slender wings,
Who cannot sing the Cardinal song, Joy
Like diamonds effervesced in sound.

The Cardinal flies. I see. Only I
Can sing the song, which only I can hear.

STEPHEN EVANS

THE TUNNEL

With every choice the ceiling slips.
You can see it if you try.
Soon the sides are within reach.
Push against them if you dare.
I tell you that they do not care.

Shift a bit and maybe you
fall forward. Drop and bend
and curl until the coming crush.
In the end we slide and slither
Down the tunnel seeking hither.

So here's the current question. Will
I bow while I am standing still?

STEPHEN EVANS

WHEN ONE IS

When one is alone, a story
One must tell can take
The place of conversation.
And yet I ask myself
To whom it shall concern?

The perspicacious wind?
The stone that stands above?
The one that lies below?
How is one to know?

My single tale is all
Bouncing off the wall.

STEPHEN EVANS

Somehow

In the evening of things, shadows lengthen.
The force of light slowly seeps away
And one can if one looks see things as they are.
For make no mistake, shadows were always there,
Hidden in the gloss of every day.

The sun has lost all interest in the world
And cannot keep its mind on daily chores
And drifts in thought to emptier spaces
And cannot remember yesterday at all,
Eternal heart fuel spent. And yet. And yet

Tomorrow and tomorrow and tomorrow,
Somehow, somehow, making, through till morning.

ALUMINUM LIFE

Shuffling alone in her aluminum life,
Gazing at the basket at the front,
The purse they bought in Italy that year
When they. When they. The purse. That year. No
In Gatlinburg, with Ann, just for the day.

Family is far away. They care
But have their own lives, mothers too.
Once a year they come and bring the kids.
At Christmas. Or Thanksgiving. One of those.
Shuffle. Shuffle. Shuffle. Shuffle. Shuffle.

In the time it takes to cross the street,
She has shuffled her entire life.

STEPHEN EVANS

PRAYER FOR A DYING TREE

What is death to a tree? What do you feel?
Standing still, strong against the wind,
What will bring you down, but time
Or men with nothing else to do but kill?
We are nations of killers.

Whom shall I invite to your funeral?
I'll be there of course. The trees around you,
Without understanding, wondering
If they will be next. For no one can explain
Why this has happened.

Heal please. Restore
My faith in earth. Amen.

RISE

I'd shake your hand but as you see
(Ha ha). My name is Mrs. Grubb.
Welcome to the neighborhood.
A new face is a joy round here.
They come and then they disappear

All the time. So welcome the new
And cherish the old, the ones who rise.
I may rise myself someday.
You'd not think so to look at me.
But still it is a possibility.

And yet I'd miss this old beguiling earth.
That's all my wisdom in a bit of verse.

STEPHEN EVANS

ABOUT THE AUTHOR

Stephen Evans is a poet, a playwright, and the author of *The Island of Always, Whose Beauty is Past Change, Prolegomena to Any New Vacation, and Funny Thing Is; A Guide to Understanding Comedy*. Find him online at:

https://www.istephenevans.com/

https://www.facebook.com/iStephenEvans

https://twitter.com/iStephenEvans

https://www.gr8word.com/

STEPHEN EVANS

BOOKS BY STEPHEN EVANS

Fiction:

The Island of Always:
> *The Marriage of True Minds*
> *Let Me Count the Ways*
> *My Winter World*
The Marriage Gift
Paradox
Whose Beauty is Past Change
The Mind of a Writer and other Fables
Some Version of This is Funny: Assorted Jokes and Jokes of a Sort
The Next Joy and the Next

Non-Fiction:

Funny Thing Is: A Guide to Understanding Comedy
Prolegomena to Any Future Vacation
Layers of Life
Liebestraum
The Laughing String: Thoughts on Writing

Plays:

The Visitation Quartet:
    The Ghost Writer
    Monuments
    Tourists
    Spooky Action at a Distance

Experience	*Three plays about Ralph Waldo Emerson*
Generations	*(with Morey Norkin and Michael Gilles)*
As You Like It	*(by William Shakespeare, adapted by Stephen Evans)*
The Glass Door	*(An adaptation of Hedda Gabler by Henrik Ibsen)*

Verse:

Limerosity
Limerositus
Sonets from the Chesapeke
The Crooked Mirror

STEPHEN EVANS

STEPHEN EVANS